KU-034-742

Dear Jim,

love from

Phil, Al and Isobel

xxx

This book belongs to

_____

A Book of Wit and Wisdom

HAPPY
50th
BIRTHDAY

Edited by Julie Mars

Ariel Books

Andrews and McMeel
Kansas City

HAPPY 50th BIRTHDAY

FRONTISPIECE BY JUDITH A. STAGNITTO

ISBN: 0-8362-3093-0
Library of Congress Catalog Card Number: 94-71129

HAPPY
50th
BIRTHDAY

Introduction

It's your fiftieth birthday! Congratulations! You've made it through those turbulent forties, so now you can reap the rewards. People in their fifties report that life in that decade is not at all what they had expected—*it's much better!* Half a century's worth of wit, wisdom, experience, and insight will have pre-pared you for anything! Celebrate the transition with this little book. It'll make you smile . . . and feel proud to be your age.

After a man is fifty, you can fool him by saying he is smart, but you can't fool him by saying he is pretty.

— E. W. Howe

Everything got better after I was fifty.

— A. J. P. Taylor

9

The age of a woman doesn't mean a thing. The best tunes are played on the oldest fiddles.

—*Sigmund Engel*

Just remember, once you're over the hill you begin to pick up speed.

—*Charles M. Schulz*

Youth, large, lusty, loving —youth
full of grace, force, fascination,
Do you know that Old Age may come
after you with equal grace, force,
fascination?

—*Walt Whitman*

There is more felicity on the far side of baldness than young men can possibly imagine.

—*Logan Pearsall Smith*

Old boys have their playthings as well as young ones; the difference is only in the price.

—*Benjamin Franklin*

A man shouldn't fool with booze
until he's fifty; then he's a damn fool
if he doesn't.

—*William Faulkner*

Age is like love, it cannot be hid.

—*Thomas Dekker*

For twenty years man grows; for twenty he blooms; for twenty he stands still; and for twenty he fades away.

—*Flemish proverb*

At fifty a man can be an ass without being an optimist but not an optimist without being an ass.

—*Mark Twain*

I don't worry about getting old. I'm old already. Only young people worry about getting old.

—*George Burns*

I am in my fifties, and looking forward to the first glimmerings of the approach to the beginning of the first foothills of early middle age.

—*Frank Muir*

It takes a long time to become a person.

—*Candice Bergen*

. . . the Indian summer of life should be a little sunny and a little sad, like the season, and infinite in wealth and depth of tone—but never hustled.

—*Henry Adams*

Growing old is no more than a bad habit which a busy man has no time to form.

—*André Maurois*

Do you count your birthdays
thankfully?

— *Horace*

Youth is cause, effect is age; so
with the thickening of the neck we
get data.

— *Djuna Barnes*

Now see here! I cut my own hair. I got sick of barbers because they talk too much. And too much of their talk was about my hair coming out.

—*Robert Frost*

The hardest years in life are those between ten and seventy.

—*Helen Hayes*

After a certain age, the more one becomes oneself, the more obvious one's family traits become.

— *Marcel Proust*

Youth is confident, manhood wary, and old age confident again.

—M. F. Tupper

We grow with the years more fragile in body, but morally stouter, and can throw off the chill of a bad conscience almost at once.

—Logan Pearsall Smith

Ah, what shall I be at fifty
Should Nature keep me alive,
If I find the world so bitter
When I am but twenty-five?

—*Alfred, Lord Tennyson*

The character we exhibit in the latter half of our life need not necessarily be, though it often is, our original character, developed further, dried up, exaggerated, or diminished: it can be its exact opposite, like a suit worn inside out.

—*Marcel Proust*

He who at fifty is a fool,
Is far too stubborn grown for school.

—*Nathaniel Cotton*

I refuse to admit that I am more than fifty-two, even if that does make my sons illegitimate.

—*Lady Nancy Astor*

When I was twenty, forty-five seemed an intolerably venerable age, an age to retire to one's countryseat and have a last long love affair with one's garden. Now that I have reached that venerable age, it seems if not the quintessence of youth then at least nowhere close to middle age—whatever that might be.

—*Erica Jong*

Age does not give sense, it only makes one go slowly.

—*Finnish proverb*

In spite of every sage whom Greece
    can show,
Unerring wisdom never dwelt
    below;
Folly in all of every age we see,
The only difference lies in the
    degree.

—*Nicolas Boileau-Despréaux*

Some men mellow with age, like wine; but others get still more stringent, like vinegar.

— *Henry C. Rowland*

If you persist to the threshold of old age—your fiftieth year, let us say—you will be a powerful person yourself, with an accretion of peculiarities which other people will have to study in order to square you. The toes you will have trodden on by this time will be as sands on the seashore.

— *Francis Macdonald Cornford*

To be interested in the changing seasons is, in this middling zone, a happier state of mind than to be hopelessly in love with spring.

— *George Santayana*

At age fifty, every man has the face he deserves.

— *George Orwell*

Nature gives you the face you have at twenty; it is up to you to merit the face you have at fifty.

— *Coco Chanel*

You've heard of the three ages of man—youth, age, and "you are looking wonderful."

— *Cardinal Francis Joseph Spellman*

34

It is always in season for old men to learn.

— *Aeschylus*

By the time we've made it, we've had it.

— *Malcolm Forbes*

Anybody can get old. All you have to do is go on living.

— *Groucho Marx*

Youth ends when we perceive that no one wants our gay abandon. And the end may come in two ways: the realization that other people dislike it, or that we ourselves cannot continue with it. Weak men grow older in the first way, strong men in the second.

— *Cesare Pavese*

Forty is the old age of youth; fifty is the youth of old age.

—*French proverb*

He that is not handsome at twenty, nor strong at thirty, nor rich at forty, nor wise at fifty will never be handsome, strong, rich, or wise.

—*George Herbert*

Within, I do not find wrinkles and used heart, but unspent youth.

—*Ralph Waldo Emerson*

A man is as old as his arteries.

—*Thomas Sydenham*

I think your whole life shows in your face and you should be proud of that.

—*Lauren Bacall*

Youth is so sure the rules have changed. Age is sure they haven't. Youth feels it knows how far it can go. Age is deeply aware of the danger. Youth feels it can always apply the brakes in time to save itself. Age knows it isn't always so.

— *Richard L. Evans*

Perhaps one can at last in middle age, if not earlier, be completely oneself. And what a liberation that would be!

—*Anne Morrow Lindbergh*

Years know more than books.

—*Proverb*

42

The years between fifty and seventy are the hardest. You are always being asked to do things, and you are not yet decrepit enough to turn them down.

—*T. S. Eliot*

No spring, nor summer beauty
  hath such grace,
As I have seen in one autumnal
  face.

—*John Donne*

When you become senile, you won't know it.

—*Bill Cosby*

The denunciation of the young is a necessary part of the hygiene of older people, and greatly assists the circulation of their blood.

—*Logan Pearsall Smith*

At fifty years, 'tis said, afflicted citizens lose their sick headaches.

—*Ralph Waldo Emerson*

I have enjoyed greatly the second blooming that comes when you fin-ish the life of the emotions and of personal relations; and suddenly find—at the age of fifty, say—that a whole new life has opened before you, filled with things you can think about, study or read about. . . . It is as if a fresh sap of ideas and thoughts was rising in you.

—*Agatha Christie*

There are people who are beautiful in dilapidation, like old houses that were hideous when new.

—*Logan Pearsall Smith*

It haunts me, the passage of time. I think time is a merciless thing. I think life is a process of burning oneself out and time is the fire that burns you. But I think the spirit of man is a good adversary.

—*Tennessee Williams*

If wrinkles must be written upon our brows, let them not be written upon the heart. The spirit should not grow old.

—*James A. Garfield*

Life is half spent before we know what it is.

—*Proverb*

A man is still young so long as women can make him happy or unhappy. He reaches middle age when they can no longer make him unhappy. He is old when they cease to make him either happy or unhappy.

— *Anonymous*

When I was young, I was told: "You'll see, when you're fifty." I am fifty and I haven't seen a thing.

—*Erik Satie*

Put an old cat to an old rat.

—*Proverb*

To know how to grow old is the masterwork of wisdom, and one of the most difficult chapters in the great art of living.

—*Henri-Frédéric Amiel*

You know how you tell when you're getting old? When your broad mind changes places with your narrow waist.

— *Red Skelton*

On his bold visage middle age
Had slightly press'd its signet sage,
Yet had not quenched the open truth
And fiery vehemence of youth;
Forward and frolic glee was there,
The will to do, the soul to dare.

— *Sir Walter Scott*

I'm at the age where food has taken the place of sex in my life. In fact, I've just had a mirror put over my kitchen table.

— *Rodney Dangerfield*

You seldom see an older person going bananas in a slow, crowded elevator.

—*Phillip Berman*

The mark of the immature man is that he wants to die nobly for a cause, while the mark of the mature man is that he wants to live humbly for one.

—*Wilhelm Stekel*

The man who views the world at fifty the same as he did at twenty has wasted thirty years of his life.

—*Muhammad Ali*

In growing old, one grows more foolish and more wise.

—*Francois de La Rochefoucauld*

Middle-aged rabbits don't have a paunch, do have their own teeth and haven't lost their romantic appeal.

—*Aurelia Potor*

Fifty years old, 212 fights, and I'm still pretty.

—*Muhammad Ali*

All sorts of allowances are made for the illusions of youth; and none, or almost none, for the disenchantments of age.

—*Robert Louis Stevenson*

At ten, a child; at twenty, wild;
At thirty, tame if ever;
At forty, wise; at fifty, rich;
At sixty, good, or never.

— *Anonymous*

I don't believe one grows older. I think that what happens early on in life is that at a certain age one stands still and stagnates.

—*T. S. Eliot*

When grace is joined with wrinkles, it is adorable.

—*Victor Hugo*

When a man is young, he writes songs; grown up, he speaks in proverbs; in old age he preaches pessimism.

— *Hebrew proverb*

In old age . . . we are like a batch of letters that someone has sent. We are no longer in the past, we have arrived.

— *Knut Hamsun*

For age is opportunity no less
Than youth itself, though in another
dress,
And as the evening twilight fades
away
The sky is filled with stars, invisible
by day.

— *Henry Wadsworth Longfellow*

Fifty is a nice number for the states in the Union or for a national speed limit, but it is not a number that I was prepared to have hung on *me*. Fifty is supposed to be my *father's* age. . . .

— *Bill Cosby*

I have always felt that a woman has the right to treat the subject of her age with ambiguity until, perhaps, she passes into the realm of over ninety. Then it is better she be candid with herself and with the world.

—*Helena Rubinstein*

By the age of fifty you have made yourself what you are, and if it is good, it is better than your youth.

—*Mayra Mannes*

It is a mistake to regard age as a downhill grade toward dissolution. The reverse is true. As one grows older one climbs with surprising strides.

— *George Sand*

You Know You're Over Fifty When...

- you feel worn out from driving your golf cart.

- you can't remember why you dreaded turning forty.

- nobody remembers the movie star you think you look like.

- you can't name three night-clubs you've been to in the past decade.

- you don't even bother to pick up the neighborhood aerobics class schedule anymore.

- the stuff your kids listen to doesn't even sound like music to you.

- your spouse doesn't suspect you of anything if you stay out late.

- you discover you've lost interest in your vices.

- all you exercise is caution.

- you find yourself starting sentences with "When I was a kid . . ."

- you find yourself thinking that a lot of people look young despite their gray hair.

- the only glint in your eyes is the sun reflecting off your bifocals.

• you feel like the morning after the night before . . . and you haven't been out the night before.

• young people presume that age has brought you wisdom.

• everybody in the "before" and "after" makeover ads looks younger than you.

Fifty-ish Things To Do On Your Fiftieth Birthday

• Fill in a blank map with the names of all fifty states.

• Donate fifty dollars to your favorite charity.

• Visit the fiftieth state to join the Union—Hawaii.

- Indulge in a sinfully expensive dinner and split the cost fifty-fifty with your dining partner.

- Put a fifty-dollar bill in a savings account. In ten years, check to see how much interest it's earned.

- Go to the local department store and see what you can buy for fifty cents.

- Visit the fiftieth floor of a skyscraper and consider how far you can see in all directions.

• Take a drive in the country and keep your speed to fifty miles an hour.

• Make a list of fifty lessons life has taught you and give it to your child or another young person.

• Bet someone fifty dollars that you can double the number of candles on your cake and still blow them all out.

Gifts for the Fiftieth Birthday

• fifty John F. Kennedy half-dollars

• a trip to Florida to reenact Ponce de Leon's search for the Fountain of Youth (He was fifty-three at the time.)

- a ride in a hot-air balloon

- a gold medal for perseverance

- a collection of the best rock and roll albums from the 1950s

- a Happy Birthday message and a baby picture displayed on a fifty-foot billboard

- a selection of brochures from idyllic retirement communities

• one perfect long-stemmed rose a week, for fifty weeks

• a set of fifty-year-old encyclopedias—just to show you're not obsolete by comparison!

This text of this book was set in
Stempel Schneidler and the display
in Kaufmann, using Quark Xpress
and Adobe Illustrator.

Book design, illustrations, and
typesetting by

JUDITH A. STAGNITTO